the dinosaurs diwali adventure

jay anika

this book belongs to

....

Today the dinosaurs are at the village market. They are busy buying lots of goodies.

Today is Dhanteras, the day of fortune. It is good luck to buy things on this day.

Meena picked some dazzling gold earrings. Rav bought a book about astronauts. Aruna chose a sparkly scarf. Bodhi found a lovely red car. Jay decided on some silver spoons (he could eat his favourite ice cream with them).

The dinosaurs were all very excited with their purchases. They went to show Maahesh. He was the wisest old wooly mammoth in the land.

"Goddess Laakshmi will bless us with lots of money and gold now," said Bodhi excitedly.

Maahesh chuckled. "Laakshmi will only show herself if you work hard and show virtue and bravery," he replied.

"My mom said that it is a time to replace feelings of greed with generosity," Rav added.

"Yes, that is right. Before you go, remember one last thing: Today was also the day that Dhanvantari came out of the ocean with the gift of Ayurveda," said Maahesh.

"What is Ayurveda?" asked Meena.

"Herbal remedies, yoga, meditation. Ayurveda is the science of life. It teaches us how to use our minds to help heal our bodies. It means we can lead a happy, healthy life and live longer," Maahesh answered.

"I would rather have all the health in the world than all the gold in the world," said Jay.

"Yes, same here. What would be the point of being the richest dinosaur in the land if you were unfit?" agreed Aruna.

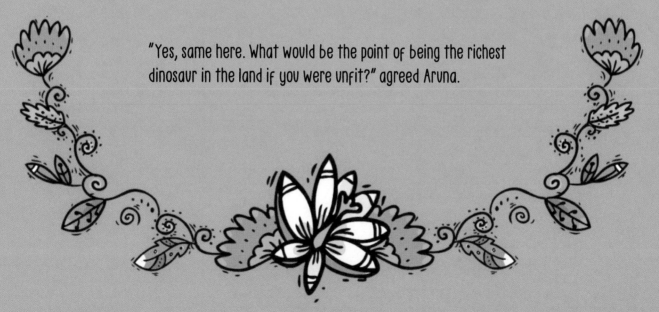

"I want all the gold and all the health," joked Rav. Maahesh and all the dinosaurs laughed.

"We will make sure we all pray for health as well as wealth so we can all live to be 201 like you!" said Bodhi cheekily.

"Hey!" laughed Maahesh. "I'm not 201, I'm only 172!"
The dinosaurs smiled and left to get back home. This week would be very busy; they needed as much rest as they could get.

The next day, the girls woke up extra early and had lovely warm baths. Today was Naraka Chaturdashi, the second day of celebrations.

Meena and Aruna were busy making beautiful rangolis out of flowers and rice.

Rav, Bodhi and Jay came to see what they were doing.

"Wow, they are amazing," said Rav.

"Today is the anniversary of the day that Lord Krishna slayed the demon Narakasura," said Bodhi while pretending to hit Jay with a stick.

Pretending to be Narakasura, Jay fell to the floor.

"Why do we celebrate him getting defeated, though?" asked Meena.

"Because Narakasura only realized right at the last minute of his life that he had the power to choose if he would be good or bad in his life. He wanted the world to remember that," replied Aruna.

"His last wish was that we celebrate the end of all the negativity he brought, because in his final moments, the new light was shown to him. He wanted to bring this light to everyone," added Rav.

"It is a great time to reflect on our behavior and think about positive changes we can make in our lives," said Jay.

Meena and Aruna continued to make their beautiful rangolis while the others went off to prepare for Diwali.

Rav woke up very excited the following day. It was Diwali, his favorite day of year! He loved all the lights and the fireworks.

The dinosaurs collected as many diyas as they could in preparation for the evening festivities.

Maahesh would get the fireworks and sparklers for the party.

That evening, Maahesh's home was transformed. It was a magical sight. Diyas lit up the pathway to his cave.

After their bellies were full, Maahesh told the most famous story of Diwali like he did every year: that of Rama and Sita.

All the dinosaurs were excited. This was their favorite story.

"I wish I was like Hanauman. He was so brave," said Kav.

"Did you know he could run at super speed and jump so high that he could reach the sun!?" exclaimed Meena.

"And he could make himself taller than the mountains," said Bodhi.

"And as small as an ant!" added Meena.

Maahesh was thrilled that they had all enjoyed the story so much.

"Now, who wants sparklers?" asked Maahesh.

"Me, me, me!" shouted the dinosaurs.

It was time for the spectacular firework show.

"What better way to celebrate the fact that light triumphs over dark and good always wins over evil," Maahesh said to himself.

The day after Diwali, all of the village collected lots of delicious food. It was Govardhan Puja.

Bodhi had made some delicious cakes and sweets. Rav had brought the greenest leaves he could find. Jay and Meena brought nuts, and Meena had made spicy rice and rotis.

All of the dinos made a gigantic mountain with all the food.

"Why do we need to make a mountain?" asked Rav.

One of the older aunties heard his question and answered.

"Many years ago, Shri Krishna lifted Govardhan Hill to protect the villagers from floods. This shows us that if we put our trust in God, he will help us in times of need. We all pray and give thanks and show how grateful we are. The mountain of food is a symbol for this."

Rav smiled and gave thanks to the older dinosaur. He continued to put more food on the mountain.

He was very grateful to be healthy and have loving friends and family. He gave thanks to God for all the luck he had been blessed with.

There was one last day of the festivities, Bhai Dooj.

Aruna loved this day. It was when all the dinosaurs, with their brothers and sisters, showed each other how much they loved and cared for one another.

Aruna woke up extra early and prayed for her brother. She put a tikka on his head and gave him some sweets.

Jay had made the most amazing chocolate cake for his sister, and he gave her the biggest teddy bear she had ever seen.

They met up with their other friends who didn't have brothers or sisters yet. Meena and Jay decided to host their own special Bhai Dooj picnic to show these friends how special they were to them. The dinosaurs all ate some yummy gulab jamun, jalebis and ras malai.

They spoke about all the fun they had this Diwali and started to make plans for next year.

Made in the
USA
Monee, IL